Thrive

A THIRTY DAY JOURNEY FOR
MOMS AND TEENS OF GROWING CLOSER
WITH GOD AND WITH ONE ANOTHER

Tina and Faith Tatum

Tatum Publishing
MEMPHIS, TN

Copyright © 2017 by Tina and Faith Tatum.

All rights reserved. No part of this publication may be reproduced, distributed or transmitted in any form or by any means, including photocopying, recording, or other electronic or mechanical methods, without the prior written permission of the publisher, except in the case of brief quotations embodied in critical reviews and certain other noncommercial uses permitted by copyright law. For permission requests, write to the publisher, addressed "Attention: Permissions Coordinator," at the address below.

Unless otherwise indicated all scriptures are taken from the New Living Translation Version of the Bible.

Tatum Publishing
12 W. Commerce Street, #852
Hernando, MS 38632
www.tinatatum.com

Book and Cover Design: Ambicionz
www.ambicionz.com

ISBN: 978-1-7329148-0-3

Thrive/ Tina and Faith Tatum. —1st ed.

Contents

Your Guide to Thrive 1

Loving God With All of Me 3

Loving Self 11

Loving Others 17

Choose Joy 23

Change 29

Fully Dressed 35

Buttons 41

Created in his Image 47

Created for His Purpose 55

Quiet Time 61

A Grateful Heart 67

Trials 73

To Date or Not to Date (Boundaries) 79

Let it Go (Forgiveness) 85

Anger 91

Fight Right 97

Living Long, What Honor Will Do For You 103

Kindess 109

Modest is Hottest 115

Friendship 121

Chit Chat 127

Don't Judge 133

Getting Social	139
Mrs. Right	145
A Servant's Heart	151
The Rock Won't Move	157
Golden Rule	163
Anxiety	169
God's Got It	175
All In	181
Continuing to Thrive	187
About the Authors	191

Above all, I would like to thank Jesus who has given my Mom and me this beautiful opportunity to minister into the lives of many other mothers and daughters.

To my Mom who encouraged me and basically made this book happen. Also, thank you for being my biggest fan and #1 mentor. I love you!

And to my Dad, who loves us and leads us like Christ does every day of my life! Thanks Pops, Love you!

Faith Tatum

To my God, Jesus, thank you for not leaving us on our own, but being an ever present help in this life!

To my one and only daughter, Faith Marie, you are all that we prayed for and more, a kind soul, genuine and true. Your love for Jesus inspires me daily. Thank you for your commitment to this journey! I Love you and I am honored to be your Mom!

To the love of my life, Alan, thank you for your love and wisdom and for always supporting our crazy dreams!

To my Mom, Alita Mitchell, as I have grown over the years, and became a mother, I have seen all of your love and sacrifices you've made for our family. Thank you for keeping us rooted and grounded in love.

Tina Tatum

Your Guide to Thrive

First let me say Thank You and Congratulations!!!! You have done what most won't. You have seen the value in investing in your relationships! In THE most important relationship, that of you and your Savior! Secondly, you have also seen value in investing in the relationship with your Mom or teenager or soon to be teen.

God created us to Thrive within the context of community in real, authentic relationships!

Here is what you will find in this book to help you do so over the next 30 days!

- Thirty topics that range from your relationship with God, each other and the people and world around you! Subjects like identity, purpose, anger, friendship, honor, forgiveness and so much more!
- Daily Scriptures that speak to the day's topic.
- Daily thoughts written by both Mom and Teen (Tina and Faith).
- Digging Deeper sections, with questions and challenges for you to take what you have read, apply and talk about together, this also includes a journaling section where you can write as you reflect on what you are personally challenged with or encouraged by.
- Doodle / Big girl coloring page with the thought or scripture for the day! Grab some colored pencils and just lose yourself in some creative time. Allow the Holy Spirit to speak to you as you speak the scripture aloud.

- Feel free to invite another friend or mom/daughter team to join you in the journey!
- Let us hear from you!!! Share your thoughts, doodles or photos of yourselves on this journey by using #30days2thrive.

You will also find each day's entry to be real and raw from both of our perspectives. And there will always be a challenge for you to NOT necessarily do things our way ... but the way of the Word, Our Savior ... Jesus ... with the sweet presence and perfecting power of the Holy Spirit to guide you to not just survive, but to THRIVE!

Thanks for going on this journey with us!

Feel Free to stay connected with Tina on Facebook at Tina Tatum Ministries and with Faith on Instagram at @thrivetheministry.

Day One

Loving God with all of Me … Growing Deep

"My mission in life is not merely to survive, but to thrive; and to do so with some passion, some compassion, some humor, and some style."

— Maya Angelou

Teen Jake

I think loving God with all of your heart involves a plan, a plan to make time. Make time for your "quiet time" with the Lord. What I mean by quiet time we will talk about in another chapter, but mostly, it's allowing time to hear from God and for your relationship with him to be cultivated; it's really a matter of the heart. Plan your life around your quiet time and not your quiet time around your life. Allow your relationship with God to pour over into your life in a positive way instead of allowing your life to affect your relationship with God in negative way.

With that being said, allowing your relationship with God to flow from your heart and affect every other area of your life, loving God with all your strength is presenting everything about you to the glory of God. It doesn't matter if it's your physical work, your talents or your brain power, in academics or school work, dedicating who we are and what we "do," is how we love Him with all of our strength!

Loving God with all your soul and mind, to me, is seeing the world and responding to it, through a Christian worldview using a ***"God shaped lens."*** Meditate on God and see everything in your life how HE wants you to see it.

For instance, listening to music; when we listen to lyrics, we are meditating on them. Ask yourself …"Is what I am listening to and repeating, honoring God?" I mean, are we singing about stuff that is not helping us grow closer to God? Are the lyrics nasty and disrespectful? When I listen to music I think about that. There is this song called "Surrender" by Natalie Taylor that I really like. It is about a boy / girl relationship, but when I hear it I think, "Hey, this sounds like how I surrendered to Jesus". So now every time I hear it, even though it's a secular song, I set my heart and mind on my relationship with God. I think this is how we can love God with all that we are … Include him in all you do and all that you are becoming; allow your life to be filtered through His heart and plans for your life.

> *Let your roots grow down into Him, and let your lives be built on Him. Then your faith will grow strong in the truth you were taught, and you will overflow with thankfulness.*
>
> – Colossians 2:7 (NLT)

Mom Moment

Since I first became a believer, almost 20 years ago, I found this scripture to be the core of keeping my relationship on track with Jesus. Through the ups and downs of life, through seasons of plenty and seasons of great need, through loss and through times of great joy and blessing, whether good or bad. I've asked myself. "Do I love HIM just as much? Am I following him just as passionately 20 years later, as I was in those first years, in what I call the 'honeymoon season'?"

Love God with all of my heart, soul, mind and strength! Some may say "Wow that's a big charge!" To which I say, "Just authentically give Him all that you are, in every area, every breath, stop holding back and it will flow like water!"

The Bible says:

> *"For in Him we live, and move, and have our being."*
> Acts 17:28

I love this verse because it doesn't separate who we are from how we live or how we "move" (do life). You see, God is not a compartmental God. He wants all of you!! I heard it once said "God doesn't want just weekend visitation (only going to church), He wants full custody (all of you)"

I am so thankful that we serve a God who pursues us, and one in whom our children need to see us pursuing / loving Him with all that we are in every situation and in every season of life! You see, God first loved us!!! This love affair is actually not of our doing and making. It is God's; He loves us with an everlasting love and pursues us in that love! (1 John 4:19), "He first loved us"). I AM SO THANKFUL, that I was on His mind long before He was on my mind. I messed myself up, and sometimes, to this day I'm messed up, and He has been there loving me all along. Now, I don't know about you, but what man, what other God, loves us as much at our worst as He does at our best?? That alone is an attribute of God that draws my heart to want to love Him more, to love Him with all that I am!!!

Our teens, for that matter, this world, are looking for an authentic, true blue, never changing, strength that they can put their hope in. Do you want a love that is consistent and goes beyond our natural bents? Do they see this modeled in our lives? I am not saying perfection, I'm simply asking, "Are we loving Him so well that others see our lives as a tangible expression of His love for them?"

Loving God with all that we are, spirit, soul, mind and body, will empower us to love ourselves and to love others in a way that will have lasting impact, and in a way that we will one day hear "well done".

Digging Deeper

Are there any areas of your life where you are holding back from your relationship with God?

_____
_____
_____
_____
_____
_____
_____

In what ways, do you "Love God with all that you are?"

_____
_____
_____
_____
_____
_____
_____

Thoughts and Prayers

_____
_____
_____
_____
_____
_____
_____

He answered,
"Love the Lord your God with all your
heart and with all your soul and
with all your strength and
with all your mind." And,
"Love your neighbor as yourself."
— Luke 10:27

Day Two
Loving Self

Teen Take

I think every teenage girl struggles with really loving herself. There is so much pressure to look good and to be something. Often times, we equate "looks" and "popularity" or "success" with love. Every girl wants to look like a movie star or model. The world, media, and movies bombard us with images of what beauty is and it's all external. So often, we look in the mirror and equate what we see with what the world values or says is worth loving. We think, if we can like what we see in the mirror, then maybe we will just begin to love it. And that's just not true.

My Mom once asked me "how can you love a God that you can't see, if you can't love the things you can see?" That question really made me stop and think. We often confuse loving ourselves with how we "feel" about our body image.

One summer I went to a youth event at The Ramp, in Hamilton Alabama, and heard Jason Vollotton talk about this very issue. He suggested getting up every day, looking in the mirror and saying what God says about you, his creation. Say, "I am created in God's image," "I am beautiful," "I am worthy to be loved," "Jesus loved me so much He died for me." Even though you may not "feel" it or believe it in the beginning, you will eventually begin to believe it because faith comes "by hearing the Word of God" (Romans 10:17). So the more we say what God says about us and the more we hear it, we will begin to have faith in it, and we will believe we are worthy of love.

So take a step back, and take a look at the very image of God himself created in YOU. It might just change the way you see everything!

> *"Self-love has very little to do with how you feel about your outer self. It's about accepting all of yourself."*
>
> - Tyra Banks

Mom Moment

We decided to stay on this scripture for three days in the very beginning days of our Thrive journey for a very specific reason. Loving God, loving self and loving others in our key scripture, which Jesus summed up as being the greatest command and the ONE, well three things for the purpose of this devotional that everything else in life hangs on!!

Some would argue that the Gospel is not a proponent of "self-love," pointing to scriptures that speak of "laying down one's life for a friend" (John 15:13), "not esteeming ourselves more highly than others" (Philippians 2:3) "for the joy set before Him Christ endured the cross" (Hebrews 12:2). All indicating, some would reason, that we should love others more than ourselves. To husbands there is even instruction to "love your wife as Christ loved the church, giving Himself for her." (Ephesians 5:25.) Then it goes on to say in verse 28-29, "So husbands ought to love their own wives as their own bodies; he who loves his wife loves himself. For no one ever hated his own flesh, but nourishes and cherishes it, just as the Lord does the church."

Our challenge in this segment of "loving self" is not to exalt ourselves, individually above anyone, but rather to see the value in all that God has created. As Mothers and Fathers, if we take care of ourselves, "nourish and cherish" this temple, this representation of our creator, we will in turn be healthy enough, spiritually, emotionally and physically to love others well.

Loving oneself is not an "either / or," rather it is a "both / and". Could it be that the "love your neighbor **as yourself**" was not a command, but rather an understanding that we would love ourselves, just as He created us, to be a precursor for being able to love ALL that He created!

Personally I believe that if we are the only creation "created in His image," and when He was finished creating us He said it was "very good", our Heavenly Father wants us to love every member of the family, including ourselves!

So Moms, take care of yourselves! No matter what you have been told in the past, YOU ARE LOVED! Care for yourself, your health, your wealth, your overall wellbeing so that you have a deep well to pour love from! In doing so you will have set an amazing example for your daughters to follow, one that always has a supply for others!

Digging Deeper

What is God speaking to you about "loving yourself" well?

_____
_____
_____
_____
_____
_____
_____
_____

Are there areas where you have trouble with self-love?

_____
_____
_____
_____
_____
_____
_____
_____

Talk to each other and God about it …

_____
_____
_____
_____
_____
_____
_____
_____

> He answered,
> "Love the Lord your God with all your heart and with all your soul and with all your strength and with all your mind." And, "Love your neighbor as yourself."
> - Luke 10:27

Day Three
Loving Others

Teen Jake

To me, loving others is my wanting the same for others as I would want for myself and being genuinely happy for them when they either achieve or receive more than me. And that goes totally against our culture!!!

I remember right around the time when I turned 14 years old, I was in a time of worship and the Lord showed me how I had treated a childhood friend really badly over several years. A new girl moved into the neighborhood that I had more in common with, and I had left out this other friend, sometimes on purpose or just sometimes because I thought I "liked" my new friend more. This new friendship was just easier; several times I am certain I was just oblivious to my longtime friend because I was absorbed in a new friendship. Basically it was all about ME and not my friend. By the time I realized this, we had moved and I couldn't just run across the street, ask for forgiveness and make things right. It was at this point that I really missed my childhood friend and began to understand that there really is enough love to go around for others!

You see, we are all born into sin and we all have a bent to act selfishly. This is kind of funny, but I still remember little things I would do that really showed that I loved myself more than I loved others. I remember small things, like asking my mom for an extra scoop of ice cream, just so I would have more than my friend. It seems silly now, but the way we treated others, even when we were younger, can haunt us later in life. God's kind of love is sacrificial, it always looks for the best in others, it bears up under any and all things, God's kind of love never fails! (1 Corinthians 13) And believe it or not, we can love His kind of way! Thank God for His grace and His redeeming love for us, so that we can love others better!

As we grow in loving God more, we will love what He created more. And as we love what HE created more (ourselves included) we will be able to love others more!

"Intense love does not measure, it just gives."

- Mother Teresa

Mom Moment

Loving God and loving others is the great commandment! Love is best revealed in actions. Much like our faith is oftentimes seen by our works, our faith itself works by love! "All of these things come to us by faith. But it must be faith that works by love." (Galatians 5:6)

One of the greatest inheritances we can give to our children is an authentic life lived for God, and GOD IS LOVE! (1 John 4:8)

The first place we live out this "love walk" toward others is at home. Unless you live alone or as a hermit somewhere, you will have "others" in your life, at least I hope you do! The sacrifice of loving others well always starts at home. You know it's love when you can get up ten times a night for that crying newborn, to feed, change diapers and let her/him know you are near and all is well. It is loving our spouse, or one day spouse, while setting the example for our children of what to expect in future relationships, and how to give of one's self wholly, in love and in future relationships.

Loving others is the best way to keep that "God kind of love" flowing through us. Since God loved us much that He GAVE His only son to get us back into relationship with Him, we see by His very nature - His love is unconditional and sacrificial. The truth of the matter is this … loving others well is not always convenient. As a matter of fact, it can be down right against what our flesh wants to do! But we do have a guarantee in scripture. God says, "LOVE NEVER FAILS." (1 Corinthians 13) in fact, it is the only thing that never has!

> *"Love is the only force capable of transforming an enemy into a friend."*
>
> - Martin Luther King, Jr.

Digging Deeper

Do you have any current situations where you find it hard to "love others" well?

_____
_____
_____
_____
_____

Talk to God and to each other about it.

_____
_____
_____
_____
_____

What can you do differently to look more like Jesus in this area?

_____
_____
_____
_____
_____

Journal your thoughts and prayers here:

_____
_____
_____
_____
_____
_____
_____

*He answered,
"Love the Lord your God with all
your heart and with all your soul
and with all your strength
and with all your mind." And,
"Love your neighbor as yourself."
- Luke 10:27*

Day Four
Choose Joy

Teen Take

Every day we make a choice.

You can either mope around like Eeyore, from Winnie the Pooh, complaining and drifting through life, or you can choose to have the joy of The Lord shine through you!

Even on those days when you just don't want to get out of bed or your school work is too overwhelming, your joy and your strength is to push through, knowing that the mountain in your way is just a grain of rice in the eyes of our God!

One of the ways I stay full of joy is read Psalms. I love poetry, especially in the Bible. Psalm 30:5 says "Weeping may last through the night, but joy comes with the morning." Not all of us love to see morning; I prefer to hit the snooze several times myself. But embrace every day as a gift from God, realizing that we don't have to go through this life alone, know He is with us and it is His strength that can produce the joy needed to face the day!

Maybe you received this book as a gift from someone who loves you dearly and is invested in you and YOUR joy. With gratitude for that person and for The Lord, choose joy… His joy IS your strength.

- If you are healthy - choose joy!
- If you are struggling in your health - choose joy!
- If you have lots of friends - choose joy!
- If you wish you had even one friend - choose joy, Jesus is the friend that sticks closer than a brother!
- If you dislike your school - choose joy - it could change the way you look at that place!
- If you just broke up with your boyfriend - choose joy - He probably wasn't "the one" anyway!
- If you are reading this - choose joy - you can read!

Mom Moment

This short little piece of scripture, we sing it, we have it hung on our walls as pieces of art, we can find it on t-shirts and tattoos, and we quote it on a regular basis as if it's a guarantee when we are facing hard times … "The Joy of the Lord is my Strength!"

Is it a guarantee? Well, some may beg to differ, but I would answer; "not necessarily. We must Choose Joy, just as we choose anything else."

We choose to enter into a relationship with Jesus, we choose to learn more about him, we even choose to be set free. (To allow Him to set us free.)

Pastor Rick Warren defines joy as:

> *"Joy is the settled assurance that God is in control of all the details of my life, the quiet confidence that ultimately everything is going to be alright, and the determined choice to praise God in every situation."*

God wired us all with a free will and He also wired us with a deep knowing on the inside that we can't do it alone. We just were not created that way.

We are created in His Image, the image of a tri-une God, three in one. God has never been alone; he has always had Jesus and the Holy Spirit with him. They are the supernatural Joy Team - The God head three in one.

We are made to find our greatest joy in the context of community! And in the context of healthy community, we don't just survive this life; we THRIVE in and through it!! Remember joy is a choice. Choose joy today!

"We're depending on God; he's everything we need. What's more, our hearts brim with joy since we've taken for our own his

holy name. Love us, God, with all you've got — that's what we're depending on." (Psalm 33:20-22 MSG)

Digging Deeper

In what areas of your life do you struggle to have joy?

_____
_____
_____
_____
_____
_____
_____
_____
_____
_____
_____
_____

What can you do to bring more joy into your home?

_____
_____
_____
_____
_____
_____
_____
_____
_____
_____
_____
_____

"For the joy of the Lord is
your strength."
Nehemiah 8:10

Day Five
Change

Teen Jake

When I was very young, my parents become Associate Pastors at a new church. Being there as our church grew really made it feel like home. Although I experienced a great feeling of belonging, I become caught up in how important I felt as a pastor's kid.

That church was really the only one I can remember being a part of and with my parents being in such an authoritative position, it made me feel somewhat "special." I felt like I was a little above others. I started to get caught up in who I was at the church and in my youth group rather than who I was in Christ. I found my identity in my "reputation" rather than in Jesus. When we left that church, I cried for days because I thought there was nothing better out there. Although I still consider everyone in that church community to be family and I do miss them, I had no way to know that the painful process of moving on would become one of the best things to happen to me. I had no idea that God was going to do something new and so amazing through what felt like such difficult change.

Once I got out of my comfort zone, it caused me to take a closer look at my relationship with the Lord, make some changes, and repent. Now I have an even bigger family and our current church home has just the right people and leaders to guide, teach and love me!

Sometimes it takes pushing your limits and getting out of your comfort zone to see God's greater purpose for your life!

Mom Moment

The dictionary gives these two definitions for change:

- to make radically different: or to Transform.
- to give a different position, course, or direction to.

Wow! That's exactly what Jesus comes to do in our lives!!! Change, although it may be apparent on the outside, does not begin there. The change Christ comes to make in our lives happens from the inside out. He comes to make us radically different, to transform us, to change the trajectory of our lives!

If you read Faith's very personal account of her recent change, I hope you can hear the intensity of her heart. We honestly had no idea that change would come so suddenly and so drastically. For several years that was a very "comfortable" place, however when God brings changes, they are always for our best. Like the gracious Father that He is, there is always a master plan laid out! Our job in the midst of change is to, as my Pastor friend Carmel Rich said to me, "keep your ear close to His mouth," meaning stay so close to Jesus that you hear His whisper, you hear His plan for every course change, every course correction, every radically different season of life!

I have heard it said, I have seen it countless times and I have come to believe, "People don't change until the pain of NOT CHANGING is greater the pain of CHANGING."

By our very human nature, we are creatures of habit, very few people like change. What is important is not IF change will come, but rather, WHEN. And when it does, how will we navigate through it?

Will we walk by faith setting a good example and a clear path for our children to follow? - **OR** - Will we sink into pits of fear and despair?

Will we look for the "God Stuff" going on around us as the Father creates new ways and charts new courses for us? **- OR -** Will we resist the change, and by doing so, walk aimlessly through the proverbial desert for another forty years?

Let's embrace the new things the Lord will do through every season of change within our own lives, with our spouse, with our kids, with our career, with our calling!

Digging Deeper

Do you like change or do your dread it?

_____
_____
_____
_____
_____
_____
_____
_____
_____
_____
_____
_____

What steps can you take toward embracing whatever change the Lord brings your way?

_____
_____
_____
_____
_____
_____
_____
_____
_____
_____
_____
_____

See, I am doing a new thing! Now it springs up; do you not perceive it? I am making a way in the wilderness and streams in the wasteland."

- Isahia 43:19 (NIV)

Day Six
Fully Dressed

Teen Jake

Every morning since I was little, my Mom taught me to "put on" the full armor of God. It's like getting physically dressed. I simply say out loud that I "put on" the helmet of salvation, the belt of truth, the breastplate of righteousness, the shield of faith, the shoes of peace and the sword of the spirit, which is the Word of God.

After I do that, I just feel like my morning is complete! It's a great way to start the day and to set my mind on having Christ in every area of my life.

Even though there are mornings when I feel too tired or I half-heartedly do it, I still do it, and I can really tell how it makes a difference throughout my day.

The helmet of salvation protects my mind and represents to me an anointing that stays on me all day; it helps protect my mind from the enemy! The breastplate covers my heart; the belt of truth says that I will be held together in that day by truth, and shoes of peace declare that I will be a peacemaker wherever I go. The shield of faith covers me from anything that this world or Satan would come at me with; it's our faith in Jesus that trumps everything else! And the sword of the spirit is the Word of God, our most powerful weapon in this life.

Being fully dressed in Christ and His righteousness not only makes a difference in your life but also in what others see in you and on you.

Mom Moment

Would you ever dream of allowing your teenager to leave home naked or only half clothed? Although you may think you have seen some teens half-dressed running around before, we won't go there on this day! (giggle)

You may think, "'the full armor' is something my kids just learned about in Sunday school with their little soldier costumes marching around reciting 'I can do all things, all things, all things, I can do all things through Christ who strengthens me!" (Philippians 4:13) Some get this visual and some are reading this wondering what in the world I am talking about!

Let's take a look at today's scripture. Paul was giving instruction on spiritual warfare to the church at Ephesus. Roman guard-ware would have been something very familiar to Paul with as much time as he spent in prison. He took a very familiar visual and used it to portray our real position and who our real war is with.

I will give you a little hint, the war is not with your teenager, your spouse or any other person. Your war is with a real Satan, the real enemy of your soul and his plan is to steal, kill and destroy!

Let me drop the precursor here, THE WHY BEHIND THE WHAT found in verses 10-12; "Finally, **be strong in the Lord and in His mighty power.** Put on the full armor of God, **so that you can take your stand against the devil's schemes.** For our struggle is not against flesh and blood, but against the rulers, against the authorities, against the powers of this dark world and against the spiritual forces of evil in the heavenly realms."

We all want to protect our children although we cannot always be with them. Why don't we all GET DRESSED daily before we run out the door into this crazy world?!?!

Digging Deeper

What did this chapter speak to you?

_____
_____
_____
_____
_____
_____
_____
_____
_____
_____
_____
_____
_____
_____
_____

Can you work on committing today's scripture to memory so that it is as natural as putting on your clothes daily? The easiest way I have found is to write the verse on a few index cards and place them around the house or in your car so that the verse is with you to meditate on as you go through your day.

_____
_____
_____
_____
_____
_____

FINALLY, BE STRONG IN THE LORD AND IN HIS MIGHTY POWER. PUT ON THE FULL ARMOR OF GOD, SO THAT YOU CAN TAKE YOUR STAND AGAINST THE DEVIL'S SCHEMES. FOR OUR STRUGGLE IN NOT AGAINST FLESH AND BLOOD, BUT AGAINST THE RULERS, AGAINST THE AUTHORITIES, AGAINST THE POWERS OF THIS DARK WORLD AND AGAINST THE SPIRITUAL FORCES OF EVIL IN THE HEAVENLY REALMS. THEREFORE, PUT ON THE FULL ARMOR OF GOD, SO THAT WHEN THE DAY OF EVIL COMES, YOU MAY BE ABLE TO STAND YOUR GROUND, AND AFTER YOU HAVE DONE EVERYTHING, TO STAND. STAND FIRM THEN, WITH THE BELT OF TRUTH BUCKLED AROUND YOUR WAIST, WITH THE BREASTPLATE OF RIGHTEOUSNESS IN PLACE, AND WITH YOUR FEET FITTED WITH THE READINESS THAT COMES FROM THE GOSPEL OF PEACE. IN ADDITION TO ALL THIS, TAKE UP THE SHIELD OF FAITH, WITH WHICH YOU CAN EXTINGUISH ALL FLAMING ARROWS OF THE EVIL ONE. TAKE THE HELMET OF SALVATION AND THE SWORD OF THE SPIRIT, WHICH IS THE WORD OF GOD.
EPHESIANS 6:10-17 (NIV)

Day Seven
Buttons

Teen Jake

When somebody is getting on your nerves or pushing your buttons, think about this scripture. We are crucified with Christ… soooooooo what part of us should be so touchy that we still have "buttons?"

My Mom and I are so close that we get on each other's nerves all the time. Well, Mom says that I don't get on her nerves, but she really does get on my nerves sometimes. I am just being real! Part of that is because we are so totally different. She is very loud and outspoken and I am more of an introvert. Especially in the morning!! She wakes up talking and singing, "This is the day the Lord has made…" and I just want to quietly ease into my day. Sometimes I find myself rolling my eyes and asking her to be quiet.

The thing is, just because we may be Christians doesn't mean that we aren't human. Things and people are going to get on our nerves or "push our buttons." The issue is how we choose to respond.

Usually when I am really getting annoyed, I do my best to pause, think about what is really going on and choose to not even respond.

Terri Igleheart, my former Youth Pastor, affectionately known as Mama T. says, "Our buttons or triggers (things that make us mad) are really our issues in our own heart needing to be addressed and transformed. God is gentle and kind in helping us to 'die to ourselves' and serve others."

Mom Moment

What do you do when your "buttons" get pushed? You know those feelings that go from 0 - 60 in one heartbeat.

- Do you fly off the handle?
- Do you resort to your "coping" mechanisms?
- Or do you choose to overlook?

My personal opinion of "buttons" for the Born Again Christ follower is to get rid of them!

Our key scripture says, "It's no longer I who live ... but Christ". Come on now, it's only by God's grace that we are even here! So why do we have such a hard time extending that grace to others?

Here is more insight from scripture found in Romans 7:21-24(NLT)

> *"I have discovered this principle of life—that when I want to do what is right, I inevitably do what is wrong. I love God's law with all my heart. But there is another power within me that is at war with my mind. This power makes me a slave to the sin that is still within me. Oh, what a miserable person I am! Who will free me from this life that is dominated by sin and death? Thank God! The answer is in Jesus Christ our Lord."*

YES! The answer is Jesus Christ. You see, when we are born again of the Spirit, our "spirit" is 100% redeemed, but this is not so with our soul (mind, will and emotions). IN CHRIST WE ARE NO LONGER A SLAVE TO SIN! (Romans 6) That sin (or our selfish nature) was nailed to the cross! The problem is we often times, in our busy lives, don't take the time to get our minds renewed and our hearts healed of the repercussions that sin had or has on us. So then we are still walking around with all these "buttons" or "triggers" that Christ Himself has made the way to be removed.

Whether it's a co-worker, your kid, your spouse, parent, brother or sister, that nosy neighbor, your pastor, or today it could be me that you find pushing your "buttons," ask the Lord to show you why, uproot whatever measure of sin or selfishness is there and then ask Holy Spirit to lead you in the ways of life! THEN your focus won't have to be on "managing" anything that's no longer there; i.e. buttons have been removed!

Digging Deeper

Describe below a recent situation where your parent, your teenager, or someone else in your life "pushed your buttons" and how you reacted.

_____
_____
_____
_____
_____
_____
_____
_____
_____
_____
_____

Pray and ask the Lord to reveal to you, what on the inside of you caused that reaction, and how you can respond differently the next time this happens. Discuss together.

_____
_____
_____
_____
_____
_____

I have been crucified with Christ; it is no longer I who live, but Christ lives in me; and the life which I now live in the flesh I live by faith in the Son of God, who loved me and gave Himself for me."

Galatians 2:20 (NSAB)

Day Eight
Created in His Image

Teen Jake

Do you remember the song you may have learned as a child in Sunday school or Children's church?

> "Jesus loves the little children
> all the children of the world
> red, brown, yellow, black and white
> they are precious in His sight.
> Jesus loves the little
> children of the world."

Who doesn't know that little song??? Well it holds a lot of truth. We are ALL created in His image and we are all precious in His sight!

I think it's amazing that we humans, of all things created, are the only beings created IN THE IMAGE of God!!! Think about that. We are also the only beings God was willing to give His Son for!! For He so loved the world!!! He gave us His very best to bring us back into relationship with Him forever!!

The value someone is willing to pay for something determines its worth.

We are created with intrinsic value, so much so… God bankrupted heaven for us … by sending Jesus!

So, if this is true about me and you, it is also true of others! Girls our age can be so critical and ugly to other girls who don't look the same, dress the same or whatever. As Christians we are called to a higher standard. We are to see the value in every person, no matter how different or no matter how unkind or lacking in love they are toward us. God sees them as valuable and needing of the ultimate love that can change everything! His love, expressed through us!

Or, many of us may find it easy to see the value in others but don't see it in ourselves! Remember, God does not make mistakes! Whether you are 5'8" tall, slim and athletic, or barely 5 foot, brunette with dark skin, God created you in His Image ... and He loves what He created, so you should too!

Our true value doesn't lie in our abilities, but rather in our identity as children of God!

Mom Moment

What a weighty thought. We are created in the image of God!

Don't misunderstand, as many have in our western, everything ME culture, we are not God. However we are created in His image and with His traits that are mind blowing! If we could to some measure, pass this revelation and reality on to the next generation, we could literally see the world changed for good!

God is the creator - so we are creators! Women... we actually (with some help) create other humans!!! Come on, you can laugh with me. Artists create art, chefs (and moms) create delicious meals, farmers sow seeds to create a harvestable crop. Teachers impart wisdom to create smarter students and CEO's create successful businesses. Hopefully, you get the picture.

God is Spirit - therefore we have a spirit. (John 4:24)

God is relational and wants us to be relational. There has always been Father, Son and Holy Spirit. In the verse just prior to our key scripture you will find, "Then God said, 'Let us make human beings in *our* image, to be *like us*.'" (Genesis 1:26)

God loves to communicate; therefore He made us (especially women) with the ability to do the same! In the beginning He said, "Let there be light" and so on, to Moses He spoke "I AM." Jesus Himself said:

> *"I don't speak on My own authority. The Father who sent Me has commanded Me what to say and how to say it. And I know His commands lead to eternal life; so I say whatever the Father tells Me to say."*

(John 12:49-50)

God is eternal and so are we, in Jesus! We are created to live forever; this life is but a vapor, a passageway to our eternal life

WITH God. As a matter of fact, the Bible says, "He has planted eternity in the human heart." (Ecclesiastes 3:11) Whether or not someone is a believer today or not, God himself planted within our hearts a "knowing" that there is more, a literal spiritual desire for eternity.

This very image that we have spirit, soul, and body, the very "temple" that holds Holy Spirit, has all been set in place for the benefit of us, our families, those around us, and is all for the Glory of God himself. Now, take some time to reflect on that.

Digging Deeper

Reflect on the absolute majesty of our King! How great is Our God!!!

_____
_____
_____
_____
_____
_____
_____
_____
_____
_____
_____
_____
_____
_____

Pray, journal and reflect on His greatness and on the responsibility we carry for being "Created in His Image".

_____
_____
_____
_____
_____
_____
_____

So God created human beings in His own image. In the image of God he created them; male and female he created them.
Genesis 1:27 (NLT)

Day Nine
Created for His Purpose

Teen Jake

Have you ever thought, "What am I even here for?" or "What am I created for?"

You are a Masterpiece! As we addressed yesterday, we are each created in His Image. So, if we are created in His image, He obviously created us with His purposes in mind!

Jeremiah 29:11 says, "For I know the plans I have for you," declares the Lord, "plans to prosper you and not to harm you, plans to give you hope and a future."

Even if you can't see your purpose right now, in the grand scheme of things, know that even in the small things, in the everyday things we walk through, God will reveal His purposes as you find yourself and your gifts being used for His Glory! God has a purpose for every day of your life!

Maybe some of you are very artsy and creative like me, some are very athletic, some have the gift of leadership, and some are gifted with peacemaking, while still others have the gift of public speaking. All gifts, no matter which you have been given, are rooted in spiritual purposes to benefit others and bring us peace when we are doing what He has created us to do.

I love what Pastor Steven Furtick of Elevation Church said about purpose.

> *"God has had a purpose for your life long before anyone had an opinion about your life."*

If you struggle with understanding your purpose or just want to dig deeper into how you are wired, there is a great tool called the ENNEAGRAM test. It's a great resource to help start the process of discovering your purpose.

Mom Moment

*"Everyone who is called by My name, whom I created for **My glory**, whom I formed and made."* (Isaiah 43:7)

Our purpose? To sum it up, is to bring glory to God!! Isaiah 43:7 confirms what might sound like "Christianease," but actually is the heart of God.

We bring Him the most glory when we are functioning in how and what He created us for. You see, we are each created with certain gifts! It is within the use of these gifts that we will find the most purpose fulfilled.

1 Corinthians 12 lists out for us all the spiritual gifts, but it starts by saying;

> *"There are different kinds of gifts, but the same Spirit distributes them. There are different kinds of service, but the same Lord. There are different kinds of working, but in all of them and in everyone it is the same God at work. Now to each one the manifestation of the Spirit is given for the common good."*

I love how the same God created us all, but that He is so creative, He made each one of us with unique gifts so we can operate in His purposes "for the common good".

In our social media, instant everything world we live in, often times we find ourselves seeing others fulfilling their purpose and comparing where we are in life to where they are.

Comparison is the killer of creativity!!! The One who "created" us did so on purpose and with a purpose.

So whether you are fourteen or sixty-four, whether you "feel" fulfilled in your purpose or not, it is never too late to seek the heart of God! It is never too late for His creation to bring Him glory! That purpose can be found in any season and in any sect of life. And one of the greatest purposes found on earth, I believe, is that of being a Mom!

Digging Deeper

What does "Created for His Purpose" mean to you?

_____
_____
_____
_____
_____
_____
_____
_____
_____
_____
_____
_____

Take some time to turn on some worship tunes, sit and just "be" with The Lord. Let Him speak His purposes into your life. Then, write out what you found out.

_____
_____
_____
_____
_____
_____
_____
_____
_____
_____
_____
_____
_____
_____

For we are God's masterpiece. He has created us anew in Christ Jesus, so we can do the good things He planned for us long ago.
Ephesians 2:10 (NLT)

Day Ten
Quiet Time

Teen Take

One of my favorite things about being a Christian is my knowing that God genuinely wants to hang out with me! Usually we forget that not only are we benefitting from our intimate time with God, but He LOVES that time with us as well.

The verse we used in Psalms says that God is our place of quiet retreat. Every day He is waiting with His arms wide open to spend time with you and love on you as His daughter!

Don't let daily distractions deprive you of the first and most important relationship you can ever have. Being in the Lord's presence is something we should cherish above all else as ours days go on.

In Mark 1:35-37, Jesus had gone away from the disciples to spend time with the Father. If Jesus had to do this so often, then as mere humans, shouldn't we do it even more often?

Setting time aside for times of quiet reflection also helps us to silence our souls so that we can learn to hear from God. When we learn to hear from Him in our private / alone time, it will be much easier to recognize His voice or leading when we are with our friends, maybe during times of peer pressure or when we need to make a big decision.

Our quiet time will benefit us in times where there is little quietness.

Mom Moment

As I pen the words of this "Quiet Time" segment, I am currently sitting in the most tranquil place! There is a slight breeze blowing and I'm overlooking a lake. The only thing I hear is the ripple of the water, the rustle of leaves and an occasional bird chirping. It is a literal "quiet place of retreat" on the outside.

Yet I struggle to take it all in and allow this time to settle my mind.

WHY?

Well, just a few hours ago Faith got her driver's license! It was a fun experience! In fact, she drove us out to this place for us to spend a few hours alone to pray and write. Amidst this perfect setting, my mind is still racing with thoughts of another step toward full blown adulthood for my girl!

WHAT'S NEXT?

Leaving home with friends, off to college, a place of her own, marriage, children??? Oh, my God I am almost a grandmother!!!!! EEEEKKKKKK!

STOP ALL THE VOICES!

Can you relate? Do you see how the Lord can set the table for times of tranquility, peace, and rest yet we must choose to partake? And sometimes it's a battle to even enter into that "place."

During these teen years, as Moms, it is so vital that we learn to "roll the care over to Him" (Psalm 55:22) so that we can find our place of "quiet retreat" where the Lord can "renew" us daily!

He is waiting; will we press through all the distractions to find this place?

Digging Deeper

Do you find it difficult to sit still and take time for those "quiet times" with the Lord?

_____

We all do at times. What can you do to purposefully find those times.

_____

You' re in my place of quiet retreat; I wait for your word to renew me.
Pslams 119:114 (MSG)

Day Eleven
A Grateful Heart

Teen Jake

When praying, it's part of my "routine" to just constantly say, "Thank You God for this," "Thank you God for that." Although I am truly grateful, it is very easy to get into routine and just breathe "thank you" without really dwelling on what you are doing.

Sometimes we just need to stop, look around and genuinely adore God for what He has done and sacrificed for us. Jesus went through the greatest punishment for us faulted humans so that we could simply trust Him, believe Him and have a relationship with Him.

Did you ever watch Veggie Tales as a child? Do you remember Madam Blueberry? Madam Blueberry was a very wealthy woman or fruit, in the cartoon who was never satisfied because she was never really thankful for what she had. The story ends with a poor little girl or asparagus, making a huge impact on Madam Blueberry with her song "A Thankful Heart is a Happy Heart …"

If God never did another thing for us, it would already be too much, since he has already sent us his son Jesus. For this, I am eternally grateful.

Mom Moment

Have you ever participated in a "No Complain November" challenge? I did for the first time a few years ago and was surprised that it was not as easy as I thought! I always say, "go big or go home," so I had the grand idea of putting a rubber band around my wrist and every time I complained I would "snap" it or "pop" my wrist.

Overall, I would say I am a very positive, thankful, glass half full kind of gal. I have always been an encourager and I love speaking words of life and building others up! So I had no idea that this challenge would indeed be a challenge!

The Bible says in Luke 6:45, "out of the abundance of the heart the mouth speaks," meaning who you really are on the inside will eventually come out of your mouth!

In this challenge, I was surprised to find that my ungrateful banter, negative words and downright complaining sessions did not seem to take place at work, in the community, in the company of friends, or even driving down the road. The majority of my down talk came at home around the people I love the most!!! GASP!! I love and cherish these humans!! Why would it be that I find myself ungrateful in my own home?

As Faith stated in her part, she got into a "routine" of saying "thank you" without really "thinking" about it. This can easily happen with negative words as well. At home we are pulling it all together, possibly at the end of a long day. Or maybe we are rushing out the door with all the projects, lunches, and schedules in the morning and EVERYWHERE in between! We are tired, mentally drained, and possibly hungry, spiritually and/or physically.

I challenge you to not give your family a legacy of leftovers. That last of you can often times not be as grateful as a well-rested and satisfied soul. Get a rubber band if you must!

Digging Deeper

List three things you are genuinely grateful for, things that money can't buy.

_____
_____
_____
_____
_____
_____
_____
_____
_____
_____
_____
_____
_____
_____

What is God saying to you about your level of gratitude? Chat about it together.

_____
_____
_____
_____
_____
_____
_____
_____
_____
_____
_____
_____

Give thanks to the Lord, for He is good! His faithful love endures forever. Has the Lord redeemed you? Then speak out! Tell others He has redeemend you from your enemies.
Psalm 107:1-2 (NLT)

Day Twelve
Trials

Teen Take

Take a look at Job, he was tested. He was put through great testing to prove his faith but he still stayed strong! Often, people go through situations and they want to blame God. They say, "Why did God let this happen?" or "I don't see God in this."

We all have different troubles and trials to face! Think about it, things that we may have thought were totally devastating in elementary or junior high, we can laugh about now. Some may be trivial in the big scheme of life, but at the time were crazy big to us. Today, as teens, things we face may very well be those we look back on and see that our trials really did help shape and grow us. Often times it's simply a test of faith.

God will never abandon us during hard times. He is always there watching the refining process of our faith, knowing what it will produce if we just stay true.

It's easy to praise God and have joy when things are going great; it's not always easy to do so during difficult times. But, if we are deeply rooted in Him, any storm that comes your way won't take you out!

"Storms make trees take deeper roots."

- Dolly Parton

Mom Moment

My husband, Alan, and I were having a conversation one day about a young man whom we love dearly and have been praying for, when he made this statement, "You know, all of the trials, mistakes and heartaches we went through in life shaped us and got us to a point of realizing how much we did need Jesus!" Hardship does have a way of either making you or breaking you!

In Christ, we have an incredible purpose in troubles. If we will respond to them as an opportunity rather than opposition, it can result in great joy. It will also bring an opportunity for our endurance to grow, and work at a level of maturity where we can then see life through a different lens.

It is so very hard to watch your children walk through difficulty! Mama Bear wants to come out and take over!!! Unless they are in harm's way, there are times when we need to, well, really absolutely must, step away yet remain ever present, staying close enough to help guide and direct them through new and unchartered waters of hardship and conflict. These are the places where our faith is proven.

I have heard it often said, "A faith that cannot be tested is a faith that cannot be trusted."

It is also in these times of watching our kids grow in Christ and develop their own critical decision making skills when our trust in God will grow as we fully release them to His loving care.

Digging Deeper

What current trial or trouble can you use guidance or give guidance in?

_____
_____
_____
_____
_____
_____
_____
_____
_____
_____
_____
_____
_____
_____

Can you remember going through a very difficult time in your life which produced a deeper faith in you?

_____
_____
_____
_____
_____
_____
_____
_____
_____
_____
_____
_____
_____
_____

"Dear brothers and sisters, when troubles of any kind come your way, consider it an opportunity for great joy. For you know that when your faith is tested, your endurance has a chance to grow. So let it grow, for when your endurance is fully developed, you will be perfect and complete, needing nothing."
James 1:2-4 (NLT)

Day Thirteen
To Date or Not to Date
(Boundaries)

Teen Take

For me, the most awkward part of a family get-together is when that one relative always has to ask, "Do you have a boyfriend yet?" Usually I just laugh it off and make some joke about how guys are stupid, but there really is a deeper reason.

In the verse from Song of Solomon 2:7, the Bible tells us girls specifically, not to awaken love before it is time. I truly believe that high school just isn't the right time for boys. I mean, come on, we have all seen it… the friend, girl or guy, who is dating someone different every few months. Or the one who has dated the same person for a year, then it ends with the nasty break up. Gossip is all around and friends have to choose sides, is it really worth all that? I am not saying that dating is a sin, just why would I want to begin to carry the baggage of heartache after heartache into my future and one day into marriage?

I have always thought of dating like a puzzle. Every time we "date" we give a piece of that puzzle (our heart) away. All the "I love you's" another piece of the puzzle. After high school or college and all the guys later … what's left?

Keeping myself pure before the Lord and saving myself for the right man who God has chosen for me is something I delight in being obedient to and will allow me to have a whole heart (puzzle) when the time is right. Besides, going to the school dance with your best friends is way more fun!

Mom Moment

Oh, if I had only listened to _____. You could possibly fill that blank in with "Mom" or a "mother-figure" in your life as a teen. Had I only listened! Or maybe your thought is, "Had I only had someone to tell me_____."

When it comes to dating, I could easily fill in both of the above blanks as I look back on my teen years. I cringe at the thought of my daughter going through her teen years like a ship lost at sea searching for a safe harbor.

Whether your daughter rolls her eyes at your input or clings to your side for it ... she desperately needs your guidance in this area of life!! And honestly, they all desperately desire us to care enough to have candid conversation with them.

Faith and I have always talked (age appropriate) very candidly about all of the missteps, mess ups and outright hormonally driven and unchecked decisions I made as a teen. Her Father and I have both shared the results of "awakening love before its time" through the aftermath of heartache, previous divorce's and her brother living 1000 miles away, whom she loves dearly. Our girls need to know the "why" behind the "what," "no," or the "not now."

We have made a decision as a family, that one day, at the right time and prayerfully, with the right young man, she will not "date," but rather be "courted." Being courted is a far cry from the world's description of dating. Courtship involves the entire family. It requires a conversation with Dad before any time will be spent with our most precious entrustment, our daughter. Courtship involves not just interaction with our girl, but also with our family. Courtship consists of understanding intentions. If the intention is a lifelong commitment, it's worth all that ... if not, he won't stick around long anyway. ;)

Digging Deeper

What are your thoughts on dating?

_____
_____
_____
_____
_____
_____
_____
_____
_____

Have you really put much thought into it? Or is it simply an "age" decision?

_____
_____
_____
_____
_____
_____
_____
_____
_____

Whether you have yet to date or are already in the dating scene, pray and ask the Lord for direction, strength and forgiveness if needed. Spend some time with one another in open discussion regarding the very best God has for you in this area.

If you are choosing to not date right now, find a friend who holds the same values and be one another's accountability partners.

Oh, let me warn you, sisters in Jerusalum, by the gazelles, yes, by all the wild deer: Don't excite love, don't stir it up, until the time is ripe — and you're ready.
Song of Soloman 2:7 (MSG)

Day Fourteen

Let It Go ...
(Forgiveness)

Teen Take

Have you ever tried to see how many grocery bags that you can carry in from the car? Having six to eight bags weighing you down makes it difficult to open doors, get through the doorway, etc. Although it is a funny image, it's an adequate representation of how we walk through life.

When we choose to hold on to something that has hurt us or make us angry, it adds on another "grocery bag" that just weighs us down! And when we are holding on to so much pain from the past, it's difficult or sometimes even impossible to get through that next "doorway" God has for us!

> *"Bear with each other and forgive one another if any of you has a grievance against someone. Forgive as the Lord forgave you."*
>
> - Colossians 3:13

So in your quiet time or while just praying wherever you are, ask God to take it all. Freely open your heart to forgive and to be forgiven!

His yoke is easy and His burden is light! And when we release all that "baggage," we will feel just how light it is!

> *You'll just keep crashing if you never take your eyes off the rear-view mirror.*
>
> - Lao Christopher

Mom Moment

Joel Osteen, in his book, Your Best Life Now, explains:

"We can't live with poison inside us and not expect it to eventually do us harm. Face it. Forgiveness is the key to being free from toxic bitterness. Get rid of all that poison. Don't let the root of bitterness grow deeper and continue to contaminate your life. You are not forgiving for their sake; you are forgiving for your sake."

You are forgiving so that you can be free.

"Forgive so that you can be made whole. Forgiveness is a choice, but it is not an option."

Forgiveness is one of the greatest lessons we can learn and one of the greatest principles we can model and pass on to our children. I have seen families ripped apart, businesses destroyed and destinies debunked from individuals who withheld forgiveness, which by the way is rooted in pride!

Unforgiveness says two major things. First it says that this issue or pain is bigger than our God. Secondly, it says that the person who is unwilling to forgive is bigger or more important than the situation. Look, by forgiving I am NOT saying that you have to agree with what happened or that you have to rekindle a relationship, but I AM saying that unforgiveness and all its poison is not worth all the havoc it creates in us and in our families!

So sing with me your favorite Frozen tune … *"Let it go … Let it go …"*

Digging Deeper

Are you forgiving the way the Lord forgave you?

What "bags" of unforgiveness do you need to put down?

Pray and give it all to Jesus! Now Move on!

"If you forgive those who sin against you, your Father in heaven will forgive you. But if you refuse to forgive others, your Father will not forgive your sins."
Matthew 6:14-15 (NLT)

Day Fifteen
Anger

Teen Take

Nearly everyone can probably say they've been in an argument or gotten so angry that they make some ignorant mistakes. Whether it's lashing out at your best friend or throwing something across the room, the realization and result of our spur-of-the-moment stupidity is sobering.

So what's a girl to do?

God tells us in James 1:19 to be slow to anger. Although reacting in anger to most of what life may throw at us is almost second nature, the Bible clearly tells us to slow down and look in the mirror.

No matter how hard it may be, it is our responsibility as Christians to stop, breathe, and ask yourself, "What exactly is making you angry and is this argument (or issue) worth it?"

One of the most important things to learn about anger is how to resolve it. The longer we hold on to anger, the longer it roots, the harder it is to dismiss. Besides, why give someone else that much control or power over you?

Someone once said, "Make your anger so expensive that no one can afford it, and make your happiness so cheap everyone can get it for free."

Mom Moment

Have there been times when I have gone to bed angry? Of course I have, who hasn't? Did I rest well? Of course I didn't! Can all issues be resolved in a short period of time? No, not all, however, when it comes to matters that evoke the strong emotion of anger, it's best to get to a place of peace of understanding even if there isn't immediate resolution ... especially as it relates to those relationships nearest and dearest to our heart.

We have a saying in our home, "100% responsibility," meaning that we take 100% responsibility for our actions and reactions. The truth of the matter is, the only thing we have 100% control over is our response to any given situation. When people mistreat us and there's nothing we can do about it, we get angry. We see it in our young children who are constantly on the lookout to make sure everything is fair. The gut reaction to get angry in the face of unfairness never really goes away. God's Word says that we are to control our tempers, even in the face of unfairness.

A person's wisdom makes him slow to anger, and it is his glory to overlook an offense.

Proverbs 19:11 (NET)

One of the greatest ways we can model this to our children, especially our teens, is to be real about our anger, to ask for forgiveness when we lose it and to understand their anger by extending forgiveness to them.

Therapists actually say that anger is just a mask for a much deeper issue or emotion. God gave us the emotion of anger, not for us to be ruled by it; rather, it is to be used as a guide or a light bulb if you will to help us see a deeper rooted issue. The Bible says we can be angry; we simply are not suppose it let it lead us to sin. The New King James Version of our key scripture in Ephesians 4:26 says, "Be angry and sin not."

Digging Deeper

Is there a current issue that you are angry over in your parent / teen relationship? If so write it down. Pray and then talk about it.

_____
_____
_____
_____
_____
_____
_____
_____
_____
_____
_____

If not, take this space to pray and journal on any unresolved issues of anger in your heart.

_____
_____
_____
_____
_____
_____
_____
_____
_____
_____
_____
_____

And "don't sin by letting anger control you." Don't let the sun go down while you are still angry, for anger gives a foothold to the devil.
Ephesians 4:26-27 (NLT)

Day Sixteen
Fight Right

Teen Take

Growing up in church there is no telling how many times I heard "a soft answer turns away wrath." When I was in the 8th grade, we talked about this verse for an entire week, and its meaning really settled into me.

So, I decided to use it on my mom the next time we argued, and when I did it made me almost laugh at how quickly it made her stop in her tracks!!!

It can be hard to hold back whatever mean comments in your rising fit of rage. Trust me; I have had my share of allowing my words make a fool of me! Remember, once words are said, they cannot be taken back, the damage is already done. The words or anger that we let fly in a moment can hurt a relationship for a lifetime.

When it comes to fighting right, the best path to take is always that of a peacemaker. Just because you offer peace does not mean that you are in agreement with the other person or you accept what is going on, it simply means you are taking the higher road!

Mom Moment

How to fight right is my husband's favorite topic when we do pre-marital counseling or when we teach at marriage conferences. He affectionately calls it "the art of peacemaking." As former law enforcement, I think the power of de-escalation intrigues him, and he has been an amazing mediator many times as our daughter has grown. He's helped us both to learn to sort out feelings from facts, and opinions from truth.

In our key scripture it says, "a gentle answer deflects anger" or in some translations, "a soft answer turns away wrath." I love the word gentle. Gentleness is one of the fruit of the Spirit in Galatians 5 22-23; Love, Joy, Peace, Patience, Kindness, Goodness, Faithfulness, **Gentleness** and Self Control!

Let's face it, conflict is going to arise! So why not make a decision today as to how we will respond to conflict? As parents, as leaders, will we respond as fools or with gentleness? Let's help our teenagers to deal with anger in a healthy way! Dr. Gary Smalley says, "Unresolved anger is the number-one enemy of our teen's healthy development and spiritual growth."

Here are a few tips for how to "Fight Right"

- Say what you mean, just don't say it mean
- Talk **to** the person not **at** the person
- Admit the offense - deal with the issue
- Affirm the person
- Listen - don't be preparing your next response
- Seek forgiveness
- Seek to understand rather than being understood
- Reflect tenderness
- Revisit the issue, not the anger, the next day if needed
- Be a peacemaker

Digging Deeper

Write down one to three things that have been a source of contention or concern between the two of you.

Set a time to pray and talk about each one, before there is an explosion!

"A gentle answer deflects anger, But harsh words make tempers flare. Gentle words are a tree of life; a deceitful tongue crushes the spirit. Only a fool desires a parent's discipline; whoever learns from correction is wise."
Proverbs 15:1, 4-5 (NLT)

Day Seventeen

Living Long, What Honor Will Do For You

Teen Take

The Bible says that when you honor your parents things will go well with you and you will live a long life. That sounds like a great deal to me!

To honor means to regard with great respect.

Honor is not just the way you act in front of your parents. Honoring them can also be if and when your friends are talking about their parents, you choose not to engage, that is honor. Doing a chore when you have not been asked, or helping your parents with something when you are not asked is also honoring them.

Honoring your parents can also be when they have told you NOT to do something. If you are presented with the opportunity to do that thing and you choose not to, but rather obey your parents, that's honor!

Honor doesn't just come through obedience; it is also found in integrity and rooted in humility.

Honor can even be how we behave in the community. People in general form an opinion of our parents based on the way we behave; after all they did raise us! How we treat others in authority, whether it is in front of them or behind their backs such as our teachers, our friend's parents, coaches, church leaders, law enforcement, also reflects how we honor our parents.

C.S Lewis once said, *"True humility is not thinking less of yourself; it is thinking of yourself less."*

Mom Moment

I love, love, love this scripture! My prayer is this... as we honor our parents in these older years, it will make up for all the years we caused them so much grief!!! You know I am kidding, but I kinda mean it!!! Alan and I both gave our poor parents many grey hairs and high blood pressure - I'm sure, during what I call those BS days, before salvation!

Seriously though, when I think of honor, I think of the centurion who we find in Matthew 8 asking Jesus to heal his servant. He said to Jesus, "I am a man under authority, just say the word and he will be healed" (paraphrased by me). The centurion honored the power and authority of Jesus, he then submitted to that authority, and in doing so was blessed. His servant was healed!

Recognizing and submitting to authority is one of the highest forms of honor.

As we teach or kids to submit to our authority, we are by default, teaching them to honor all authority. Of course, the opposite of that is also true. If we do not teach and model an understanding of Biblical authority, our children will neither recognize nor honor that authority throughout their lives, and that will only lead to further rebellion and hardship.

When Faith was little, and correction was needed, we would gently explain that it was our job to be the "authority" in her life and that we submitted to God's authority in teaching her. If we did not do so, we ourselves would be in disobedience to God's order of delegated authority. It's not always an easy reality, but it is the truth.

Now, back to my opening statement, as we do so very much honor our parents in these changing seasons of life, as they age and as we do as well, Faith is also learning that we never outgrow honor.

Digging Deeper

In what ways can you show honor to your parents or those who are parental figures to you?

If you have not always been very honoring, pray. Ask for forgiveness and start anew today!

If you honor your father and mother, "things will go well for you, and you will have a long life on the earth."
Ephesians 6:3 (NLT)

Day Eighteen
Kindness

Teen Take

Who doesn't love the fairytale - Cinderella? I love the 2015 Cinderella movie starring Lily James. In that movie, right before Cinderella's mom passed away, she gave her final words and instructions to the young Cinderella by saying to her, "Have courage and be kind." That instruction was something Cinderella kept with her throughout her life and was evidenced throughout the movie. You can see how it greatly affected every situation she faced.

We can look at this movie and think "how cool," "that's my new motto... Have Courage and Be Kind," but it's not only in some fairy tale, it's also in the Bible! In Colossians 3:12, we find that we should "clothe ourselves with kindness, mercy, humility, gentleness and patience."

Growing in our walk with God, we should be known for our kindness, our gentleness and our patience! Something as simple as a smile can change someone's day!

In Cinderella, even when her stepmother and step-sisters mistreated her, locked her up and lied about her, she was still able to hear "that voice" within her guiding her to "have courage and be kind." And she did! If she could withstand being treated so horribly, surely with the help of the Holy Spirit we can overcome so much more.

"Have Courage and be Kind!"
- Cinderella

Mom Moment

Kindness is not a trait we often find as a prevailing virtue in this generation. I'm talking about true kindness, not just platitudes. We live in such a busy, climbing to the top of the ladder, competitive world. Often times we are just too distracted and running at the speed of light to even have time for a kind gesture.

Miriam- Webster dictionary defines kindness as: *The quality or state of being gentle and considerate.*

Of course, we as parents, teachers, and a society in general would love to see kindness run rampant! But did you know that a recent study actually shows that how kind teens are to strangers is a predictor of how much or little trouble they will have later in life? (Greatergood.Berkeley.EDU)

Here are some of the findings:

- Not only does kindness seem to make kids happy, but it also benefits them later in life.
- Kindergarteners who are kinder and more cooperative are more likely to avoid drugs, stay out of jail, finish college, and find a job.
- High schoolers who volunteer for just 10 weeks lower their risk of cardiovascular disease.

Wow, who knew??? But, don't mistake kindness for being a doormat, or someone who is easily pushed around. True kindness carries a certain measure of strength under control. It is a great attribute to model and pass on as a spiritual legacy to our children.

"Kind words can be short and easy to speak, but their echoes are truly endless." - Mother Teresa

Digging Deeper

Thoughts and prayer:

What random acts of kindness can you show today?

Since God chose you to be the holy people he loves, you must clothe yourselves with tenderhearted mercy, kindness, humility, gentleness and patience.
Colossians 3:12 (NLT)

Day Nineteen
Modest is Hottest

Teen Take

I love the Message translation of this verse:

"And I want women to get in there with the men in humility before God, not primping before a mirror or chasing the latest fashions but doing something beautiful for God and becoming beautiful doing it."

When most people hear "modest is hottest" or "dress modestly" they think boring, drab, old lady or that they can't shop at certain stores. The Bible doesn't give us instruction on this subject just to be a downer or to be unfair; the direction the Word gives us is for our own good.

It's not that we can't style our hair nicely or wear jewelry; it's more a matter of the heart. (Humility)

It's a matter of whether or not we are wearing clothes that bring attention to ourselves. Are we wearing hoochie clothes because we want people to look at us?

I hear girls say all the time, "It's my body!" or "Why don't they just not look?" knowing full well they dressed the way they did to get "the look."

What we have to understand is that guys' brains are wired differently. They can't help but notice or look. Their brains are like cameras, taking a snapshot of every image. We are not supposed to be a stumbling block in front of others. I mean, one day when you are in a committed relationship or married, do you want images of other girls running through his mind?

We should dress in such a way that keeps our friends, our brothers in Christ from having another image to deal with. The media gives us more than enough. Let's all help a sister out, help a brother out and consider the "what" and "why" behind what we wear.

"Even if I did have, you know, a 'Sports Illustrated' body, I'd still wear elegant clothes." - Adele

Mom Moment

So what does that scripture look like in the 21st century, "modest in appearance" some would ask. Since the Word of God is timeless, I doubt trying to justify modern style or trends carries much weight with God. He is God, He does not change.

I remember the days when I cared more about others opinions and my own opinion than I did God's. And I certainly wasn't aware that He had anything to say about how I clothed myself.

Look, I am not saying you should wrap yourself up in a sheet, but I am saying that we can stay in trend and be classy! God sees real beauty from the inside out! One of the greatest ways we can model this for our teenagers is to model real beauty to them, and not give in to every single fashion trend!

We have a general guideline for dress in our home; the 3 B rule. Keep your **back side, boobs and belly** covered! No one really needs to see that! What happened to the days of a little mystery?

I love these words from "Confessions of a Teenage Bride" by Natasha Craig, a 22 year old blogger, young wife and new mom:

> *"Maybe the problem is that we are trying too hard to be hot when we need to work on being beautiful. Because, a beautiful girl, one that is physically a mystery is much more appealing in the long run than the girl who bares it all.*

There is a time and place to be hot, to be desired and to be sexy. And it's not in the grocery store, at work, or at school. A truly wonderful man, who will treat you well, and love you forever, will want you to be beautiful for the whole world to see!

But ... He will want you to be hot ... **only for Him.**"

Digging Deeper

Has this chapter offended you? If so, why?

_____
_____
_____
_____
_____
_____
_____
_____

Write your thoughts on what real beauty is. Then compare them to what God has to say.

_____
_____
_____
_____
_____
_____
_____
_____

If needed, are you willing to make a few adjustments?

_____
_____
_____
_____
_____
_____
_____
_____

And I want women to be modest in their appearance. They should wear decent and appropriate clothing and not draw attention to themselves by the way they fix their hair or by wearing gold or pearls or expensive clothes. For women who claim to be devoted to God should make themselves attractive by the good things they do.
1 Timothy 2:9-10 (NLT)

Day Twenty
Friendship

Teen Take

To feel loved and have really great friendships does not require us to have tons of friends or to have everyone want to be your friend. It's okay if not everyone in your class considers you a friend, actually that's probably kind of healthy, you don't need all that drama anyway! It's okay to have a group of close friends, people you trust and who have shown they are able to really love.

My mom has always told me that "it's ok to love from a distance." I think we sometimes put undue pressure on ourselves during these teen years thinking we need to be accepted by lots of people. Actually, Jesus Himself only had a small circle of close friends.

Some traits that I think that are important in true friendship are: loyalty, love, joy (laughter), honesty, Christlikeness, and kindness just to name a few.

One of the first Bible verses I ever learned was Proverbs 17:17 *"A friend loves at all times."*

So the question we should ask ourselves is, "are we that kind of a friend?"

I am thankful to say that I have many friends in a larger circle, but I have a few very close friends, one is my cousin. I know they are there for me and I am there for them, I love them as my sisters!

Be that friend!

Mom Moment

My, oh my! Friends and the pre-teen and teenage years!! Friendship in this period of life can either be one of the greatest joys or one of the greatest challenges of life. Well, actually it can be both filled with both joy and challenges!

How many of you moms can remember all the people in your life who were really close friends in high school? How about the friends who were there, but just not as close? Now how about all the other kids in your life who, for whatever reason, just didn't really connect with you, due to differing interests, sports or band, theater or tennis? How about those really difficult girls who always seemed to have a problem with you? Oh wait, not you, that was me, just me (giggles). Of all those people, how many are you still in relationship with today? Can you count them on more than one hand? If you can, you've beat the odds!

Most of us leave high school and college with a hand full or less of really close friendships that will last a lifetime.

As adults we have family, friends, acquaintances, colleagues, and then everyone else. Many are in our lives for:

A season, some for reasons, and very few for a lifetime.

God is calling us into authentic relationship with Him regardless of the season of life we find ourselves in, with whoever He has chosen for us to walk through life with. He calls us each to walk as a reliable friend with reliable friends ... knowing that HE is The One who will always be there as THE friend who sticks closer than any brother.

May we model for our children how to be a friend to all and may we also be a reliable, loving and trusted friend to those He has entrusted closest with us in this life.

Digging Deeper

Who are your closest friends?

_____
_____
_____
_____
_____
_____
_____
_____

If you are in need of friendships, have you first shown yourself friendly in order to have a friend?

_____
_____
_____
_____
_____
_____
_____
_____

How can you become a better friend? Pray and journal here.

_____
_____
_____
_____
_____
_____
_____
_____

One who has unreliable friends soon comes to ruin, but there is a friend who sticks closer than a brother.

Proverbs 18:24 (NIV)

Day Twenty-One
Chit Chat

Teen Jake

The most important conversations we can have are those we have with God, our Creator; He does know us best and really wants to hear from us! He wants to hear from us often; not just during times we set aside to pray, but also in our daily running around; between classes, as we take a test, when we are sitting around thinking about a situation we are facing. Directing those internal conversations to God is an important part of our communication with Him.

The way we talk to God is very important. In Bible class I learned that there is an acronym titled A.C.T.S. it's a blueprint for our prayers, which are our conversations with God. It stands for adoration, confession, thankfulness and supplication (requests). I think a lot of people just blast into prayer with just "me, me, me." This acronym can really help keep our conversation on track, and when our conversations with God become deeper than just "me" it will help us to have better communication with others, just like Loving God has the same effect.

My Mom and I communicate pretty well. We have to remember that our parents are people too! They deserve to be treated with respect and with kind words. From our time spent in conversation with Jesus we will have more of the right response for them. Remember, your Mom or the Mom figure in your life will always be there for you, they are your biggest cheerleader, so watching how we talk to them will help keep those relationships strong.

How people hear us talk to our friends, our teachers, our siblings and parents may be the very first impression they have of us and our walk with God, so make your first impression a good one. Watch that Chit Chat!

Mom Moment

Faith took a little different twist on today's subject, and I'm so thankful she did, so if you haven't read her Teen Take, please take a moment to do so.

As mothers and as believers, our "chit-chat" or conversations, if you will, carry weight and a certain amount of power. It's not that words themselves have power, but the way in which we use them and the power we give them to either bring life or death is not just a notion, it's a reality!

Faith's point of our conversation with God affecting our conversations with others is a very valid point. How much time do we spend venting to our girlfriends rather than talking to God about our issues, challenges and dysfunction?

Do our children hear us building up or tearing down with our words?

Do they hear judgments and a "holier-than-thou" tone or a grace filled message when we speak?

Do we use our upbringing or culture as an excuse for spouting off that "little Irish temper" or "Cajun spunk"? That kind of talk or anything similar is no longer valid when we are a "new creation!"

Do our passengers hear road rage or silence? Blessings or cursings? Just because it comes to our mind doesn't mean it has to come out of our mouth!

Our culture, from commercials and movies to song lyrics, glamorizes rude, crude and distasteful language. Even some Christians drop bombs as if to say "I love Jesus but I am not legalistic." The real question is, "Do my words impart grace and glorify my Savior, or do they imply that anything goes?" "Will I care that my words could be a stumbling block to those around me, including my children?" I know adults today who were raised in Christian homes, were in church every week who will not step foot back in church because they were seeing and living with one set of parents at church and another at home. We are first seen or heard by the words we use.

> *"Out of the abundance of the heart, the mouth speaks."*
> (Luke 6:45)

My prayer is that your heart is flowing with life and love so as your words flow, they will indeed be gracious and attractive.

Digging Deeper

Reflection, prayer and journal time ...

_____
_____
_____
_____
_____
_____
_____
_____
_____
_____
_____

Discuss: If your chit-chat or words you use are a problem, agree to help each other by holding each other accountable in a graceful way.

_____
_____
_____
_____
_____
_____
_____
_____
_____
_____
_____
_____

Let your conversation be gracious and attractive so that you will have the right response for everyone.
Colossians 4:6 (NLT)

Day Twenty-Two
Don't Judge

Teen Jake

Last Sunday during worship, there was a family that came in and sat down in the row in front of us. Through two songs I stood there thinking about why the family was not standing up during worship. I spent worship time dwelling on what they were doing and instantly categorizing them in my mind when I should have been focusing on the Lord. Please remove the plank from my eye now!

Sometimes the most judgmental people are the ones in "the church." They are the very ones who, having experienced the amazing grace of our God should be freely extending that grace to others! Myself included!!!

Not only is judgment wrong for us as humans, but it can turn our ear away from something God is trying to tell us or correct in us as well.

My mom has always said that when we have one finger pointed at another person that leaves the other four pointing back at ourselves.

Our Job as Christians is to first make someone feel they belong, are welcome in church and feel loved. Give them a chance to see that God is love and He is working in and through us.

Why don't we just give people a chance to belonging before they believe, not the other way around?

Mom Moment

There are some things more caught than they are taught.

What do I mean by that? We can teach our kids scriptures, we can teach them how to serve others, we can teach them how to go to church, and we teach them to say "Yes Ma'am" and "No Sir". We can teach them all kinds of things, good or bad. But what sticks with them the most is what we model, who we are in private as well as in public, those are the things that are "caught," if you will, or passed down.

Do we model what scripture teaches us in the areas of giving, loving others, forgiving, honesty, integrity, or perhaps the area of passing judgments? Do we model the 1 Corinthians: 13 type of love, by always looking for the best in others?

If ever there is a generation looking for the authentic, it is this one! Why waste time playing church, why not BE the church, a shining example of all that Christ came for and gave His life for?!?

This area of getting the plank out of our own eye (self-evaluation) before removing the speck in another's eye is one that, if we model it in humility and admit when we miss it, will set our children and our relationships up for success!

Remember that law of sowing and reaping? Some may call it karma? It holds true in this area of passing judgments on others as well. We can help get our lives and our teenagers' lives off of the proverbial "hamster wheel" by stopping the madness!!

Here is how we can help:

- Take three deep breaths before saying a word
- Ask yourself this question, "Would I want someone accusing me of this?"
- Hold your tongue
- Fix your face (our facial expressions say more)

- Admit when we miss it
- Move forward in humility

Digging Deeper

In what areas do I find myself judging others harshly?

_____
_____
_____
_____
_____
_____
_____

Could it be that I have some of those same issues in my own life?

_____
_____
_____
_____
_____
_____
_____

Ask the Holy Spirit to bring healing and humility to this area.

_____
_____
_____
_____
_____
_____
_____

Do not judge others, and you will not be judged. For you will be treated as you treat others. The standard you use in judging is the standard by which you will be judged. "And why worry about a speck in your friend's eye when you have a log in your own? How can you think of saying to your friend, "Let me help you get rid of that speck in your eye," when you can't see past the log in your own eye? Hypocrite! First get rid of the log in your own eye; then you will see well enough to deal with the speck in your friend's eye.

Matthew 7:1-5 (NLT)

Day Twenty-Three
Getting Social

Teen Jake

Sometimes when I realize that my relationship with God is drifting, I will delete my Instagram account on my phone. It's the only social media I am currently on.

People have asked me in disbelief, "Why would you do that?" or "How can you do that?" Honestly, it's just another distraction at times.

With all of my school work and everything I have to do at home, church, time with family and friends, being so concerned with what everyone else is doing can be a way of procrastinating and losing HUGE chunks of time!. When we find ourselves comparing our entire lives to someone else's "highlight" of their day, it can also be unhealthy.

We spend hours a day checking in on what everyone else is doing, concerned about who is "liking and commenting" on what we have posted, and checking out all the "current trends;" the truth is, we are really only seeing what people want us to see. We feel like we have all these friends, yet we don't really know most of them very well.

Our time spent on social media can become an idol when we care more about it and spend more time on it than we do in cultivating our relationship with Christ and with those he has given us to love, like our family!

Galatians 5:13 says,

"You, my brothers and sisters, were called to be free. But do not use your freedom to indulge the flesh; rather, serve one another humbly in love."

Mom Moment

What God creates or allows to be created always has the potential for the enemy of our souls to take, twist, and use for not so glorifying purposes. I believe one of the greatest tools to reach people in this age is social media, for great good and for great evil. Evil is not just evident from the aspect of predators or online trash, it also shows up in a more subtle way.

God's purposes for His people are always to build up, to edify and encourage, to build family, and to build unity in The Body. So, of course the enemy's tactics are the exact polar opposite - he comes to steal, kill, and destroy, he is the accuser of the brethren and the ultimate divider.

So, as it relates to the social media age of the internet we are in, I really encourage you to take time together daily and set boundaries with the times spent on line for you as a mom, and for your teens. It's for their safety and for the sake of the family. If you have not ever set boundaries in this area, it may be difficult to start now - but it is possible! Chances are you pay the bill, so that phone is yours, not theirs, technically. When we make strides to protect each other and grow together in this area, over time it will be appreciated, if not at first. Remember to always share the "Why" behind the "What".

Here are a few stats that may help us move toward a less "disconnected social - on line" to a more real "face to face social" by setting our eyes and minds on better content.

- 55% of teens have given out personal info to someone they don't know, including photos and physical descriptions.
- 29% of teens have posted mean info, embarrassing photos or spread rumors about someone.

- 29% have been stalked or contacted by a stranger or someone they don t know.
- 24% have had private or embarrassing info made public without their permission.
- 67% of teenagers say they know how to hide what they do online from their parents.
- 43% of teens say they would change their online behavior if they knew their parents were watching them.
- 39% think their online activity is private from everyone, including parents.

My prayer is that as parents we may consider real candid conversation and perhaps a "reset" for both teen and parent when it comes to how "Social will be.

Digging Deeper

Moms, share with your teens how you spent "social" time as a teenager.

_____
_____
_____
_____
_____
_____
_____
_____
_____

Teens, share any areas that you may have shown or shared too much on social media?

_____
_____
_____
_____
_____
_____
_____
_____

Do you need help backing out of some areas?

_____
_____
_____
_____
_____
_____
_____
_____

*Set your mind on things above,
not on earthly things.*
Colossians 3:2 (NIV)

*Look up, and be alert to what is
going on around Christ – that's
where the action is. See things from
His perspective.*
Colossians 3:2 (MSG)

Day Twenty-Four
Mrs. Right

Teen Take

As teenage girls, we are constantly bombarded by images of what the world thinks relationships or marriage should be like. Whether it be social media, movies, fairy tales, romantic comedies or the broken relationships, of people we know, they seem to be all around us. Can we look instead, at God's Word and the very Creator of relationships for what they should look like?

One of the things I think we, as teenage girls can do to prepare ourselves for a committed relationship is to pray for our future husband and to pray for ourselves to be "the one" some day. Many girls my age and into their early twenties sometimes pray "God send me the one" or "God, send me a husband to be like this or be like that." We pray all of our expectations of him instead of praying "God prepare ME to be the one, prepare ME to be a wife someday."

I have made a "list" of just a few things that I pray for my future husband and I thought I would share it with you. These are just a few examples.

I invite you to pray them, change them to fit your "list,"

- I pray he has a great knowledge of Jesus and will keep Him first.
- I pray God will protect his ears, his eyes and his mind and that he would have spiritual endurance.
- I pray he will resist temptation and make wise choices.
- I pray he will have a heart for me and for our children one day.

We can also pray these same virtues for ourselves as we are becoming Mrs. Right!

Mom Moment

As a wife and mother, there is no greater reward on this earth than to see Proverbs 31:28-29 come to pass. To know that you have done your best, not perfection, but your very best in serving God and your husband and children. That on earth we hear a "well done" by the quality of the relationships that are produced out of our life in Christ and that one day we will hear that "well done" as we enter eternity.

Are there days when I feel like I have totally missed it and dropped the ball on this wife and mother gig? Absolutely! Do I stay there long? NO Ma'am! Don't let the enemy play with your mind like that! Take the next step; crawl if you must, just keep moving forward!

Alan and I have both been in train wreck relationships, I may have been the lead conductor in several, with marriages that ended in divorce leaving a trail of broken people in our past. Thank God that Jesus makes all things new! And all things can work together for the good of those who love God and are called according to His purposes. (Romans 8:28).

So out of those past life experiences, combined with what we have learned about what relationships should look like according to the Word of God, we have both risen from the ashes of "what not to do." With God's grace, we are pressing on to the mark of all that marriage and all that we can be as individuals.

The key element in healthy relationships is not "finding one," there is not "one" out there, it is in "being the one." Healthy and happy relationships consist of people who are first healthy and happy as individuals. You have probably heard the old saying "two halves don't make a whole." Be all God created YOU to be, whether you are single or married, God's purpose in every season is that we are moving from faith to faith and from glory to glory, looking more like him in our own lives and in our relationships.

Digging Deeper

Thoughts and prayers ... maybe a little personal inventory (self-evaluation)?

_____
_____
_____
_____
_____
_____
_____
_____
_____
_____
_____
_____

Talk about your expectations of relationships prior to reading today's devotional. Is the Lord directing change in any of those expectations?

_____
_____
_____
_____
_____
_____
_____
_____
_____
_____
_____
_____

Her children stand and bless her.
Her husband praises her: "There are
many virtuous and capable women
in the world, but you surpass
them all!"
Proverbs 31:28-29 (NLT)

Day Twenty-Five
A Servants Heart

Teen Jake

At our church, you can volunteer to serve behind the scenes; it's called the "Dream Team." I love to work with the children and being there to love them while their parents are able to attend church and get something out of the message that is being presented on Sunday mornings. Serving in this way always gives me a great sense of satisfaction, even more so than on the days that I just "attend" church.

> **Being a part of "the church" isn't just about going to church to be served but to find a place to serve God and others.**

Serving not only applies to your parents and people who have authority in your life but also to life in general. What about holding the door open for the next person walking behind you or helping an older person with their grocery bags, or maybe even asking your teacher if they need any help?

Galatians 5:13 says, "For you have been called to live in freedom, my brothers and sisters. But don't use your freedom to satisfy your sinful nature. Instead, use your freedom to **serve one another in love.**"

Jesus Himself came to serve and not to be served… and we follow His example. If God Himself came in human form (Jesus) to serve, how much more should we be able to serve other people? It is always better to give than to receive.

"Service is the outward expression of honor."

- Alan Tatum (My Dad)

Mom Moment

The "S" word!!! Serve!

Serving runs counter cultural to our western culture "Climb the corporate ladder," "Live the American dream," "Be all you can be" selfie centered mindset. We are born into a "me" centered world. Change my diapers, feed me, burp me, hold me, rock me, me, me, me, me!!! Serving others is not found in our flesh or found in our "nature."

Recently, I heard someone say, "We are born takers but we are born-again givers." I thought, "WOW!! That is so true!"

A servant's heart is only found as we lay down life, (our own selfish ways) and pick up the way of the Cross. The way of service is found in the foundation, the roots, of the Gospel. Our key scripture tells us that Christ himself came to serve, not to be served.

The Apostle Paul went on to say:

"For what we proclaim is not ourselves, but Jesus Christ as Lord, with ourselves as your servants for Jesus' sake."
2 Corinthians 4:5 (ESV)

"Whatever you do, work heartily, as for the Lord and not for men, knowing that from the Lord you will receive the inheritance as your reward. You are serving the Lord Christ." Colossians 3:23-24 (ESV)

With this in mind, we have always made an intentional effort to model this for our daughter as well as plan opportunities for her to serve from a very young age. In every season of life we can find time for what is important. When Faith was small, she had age appropriate chores around the house, she would help pick up trash after an event a church, we would have her wait and allow others go before her in line, or help carry in bags of groceries for her grandmother. The opportunities grew as she did. Now she has grown and we have seen her desire to serve others become her very own, such as taking it upon herself to sign up to help in the nursery. I find her asking how she can help others. As a mother, this makes my heart smile, so I am certain that it makes the Lord's heart pleased as well.

As you can see that "S" word can go from a discipline to a delight if we will just take that first step in giving of ourselves!

Digging Deeper

Do you resist serving others?

_____
_____
_____
_____
_____
_____
_____
_____
_____

If so why?

_____
_____
_____
_____
_____
_____
_____

How can you (together) find a place to serve?

_____
_____
_____
_____
_____
_____
_____
_____
_____

For even the Son of Man came not to be served, but to serve others and to give His life a ransom for many.
Matthew 20:28 (NLT)

Day Twenty-Six
The Rock Won't Move

Teen Take

Have you ever been so stressed over school work that you are just paralyzed?

I have!

Just this past week, I was in a production of My Fair Lady at school. I had to be at school early to prepare for the matinees and stay late (10 pm) until the last production was over. I had chemistry test, a project due, labs, writing this devotional, orders from my Happiness Homemade business along with my responsibilities around the house ... it seemed like everything was piling on top of me!

Sometimes when I feel overwhelmed, I just stop, and don't do anything, which does NOT help matters! In fact, I get further behind and life becomes even more stressful!

Yet within the stress and craziness of this very busy week, I still found a way to carve out time for Jesus. Those few moments that I spent reading my Bible or listening to worship helped me to feel more centered throughout the week.

Besides all of the things that life throws at us ... schedules change, test dates change, people change, life changes, but God never changes!

God never changes and He is always there to hold you up and give you stability and comfort! So, lean on THE ROCK. His strength is more than enough to hold you and all you are faced with!

Mom Moment

If you are reading this with your teen, we can all honestly say "THANK GOD WE SURVIVED THE TEEN YEARS OURSELVES!" Think about it, it is the time of the most physical, emotional, and hormonal change and growth of life!

I can remember being in high school, sitting on the end of my bed and crying uncontrollably because I still hadn't decided on a major for college. It was as if my entire world was spinning out of control and if I didn't decide that very moment tomorrow wouldn't come! As I look back and laugh about it now, I am also thankful that I can be there for my daughter as she now faces her own highly emotional and life altering decisions.

Obviously, there are going to be times that our teenagers feel overwhelmed with all the changes and all the newly developing responsibilities. Perhaps you woke up overwhelmed today, with a sense of dread, with all you have on your plate or hectic schedule. Here are just a couple of things we can do, practically, to regain a sense of wellbeing:

- Take EVERYTHING to Jesus first in prayer!
- Learn to say "NO!"
- Learn to ask for help.
- Learn to move on.

God is such a great Father, that He Himself wrote our future and that of our children's lives in His book before one we were created! I take great comfort in knowing that He knows the plans He has for us - those plans are to prosper us, not to harm, plans of a hope and a future; an expected end! (Psalm 139:16, Jeremiah 29:11)

Aren't you glad that God does not change even when life and circumstances do? JESUS IS THE ROCK THAT WON'T MOVE!

Digging Deeper

When areas of your life that may seem to feel overwhelming, take them to Jesus!! Write about that here.

When my heart is overwhelmed; lead me to the rock that is higher than I.
Psalm 61:2 (NLT)

Day Twenty-Seven
Golden Rule

Teen Jake

Have you ever thought about how your own kids are going to treat you and interact with you some day? I have.

Today is about the "Golden Rule," which is treating others the way I would want to be treated. When it comes to my parents sometimes I think, "Would I want my kids to treat me this way?" or "Would I want my daughter to keep this from me?" For real! The Golden Rule doesn't just apply today, it also has far reaching impact, the law of sowing and reaping applies here as well. We can allow that to be pretty scary or we can choose to make it something we can make a difference with!

When your Mom asks you to do the dishes, take a moment to think, "Would I want my kid to pitch a fit about helping out?"

Also, if we can have our eyes open every day for those who are feeling alone, bullied, or maybe someone who has had bad day, we can make a difference! You never know what someone is going through. Smiling, saying "Hi" or asking them how they are doing can go a long way. Many times people just want to know that they are being seen. I know if I was having a bad day and someone cared enough to say something, I'd feel better.

There is enough ugly in the world, we can bring light and happiness to someone's day, it is one of the ways I would like to be treated, so I try to do the same for others.

It's been said that *"Character is how you treat someone who can do nothing for you in return."*

> *"A lot of people ask me, 'How did you have the courage to walk up to record labels when you were 12 or 13 and jump right into the music industry?' It's because I knew I could never feel the kind of rejection that I felt in middle school. Because in the music industry, if they're gonna say no to you, at least they're gonna be polite about it."*
>
> - Taylor Swift

Mom Moment

Such a simple yet profound truth; do unto others as you would have done to yourself, the essence of the golden rule.

Throughout this walk of faith and in the many roles we will fill as a mom, wife, daughter, sister, housekeeper, teacher, cook, counselor, chauffeur, nurse, Sunday school leader, youth volunteer, PTO president, business owner, scorekeeper at the ball games, hair dresser, costume designer, and overall CEO of our little universe, we can find ourselves so busy filling so many roles that often times, at the end of the day, we are spent! Take a breath!

Have you ever found yourself at the end of one ... or maybe **many** days with little left to give and frayed nerves? We all have! When we find ourselves in a season of constant pouring out we MUST make sure we are being filled, with His Word, His presence, His Love!!!

IF we do not, we will find that the very place and very people that we are called to minister to FIRST - our family - will be the ones to suffer. We can find ourselves short tempered, disengaged, too exhausted to demonstrate the "golden rule" on the home front.

So let's make a pact – we won't do quite so much "doing for others" in this race called life, or we will have little left to give and do for our family, the ones who need us the most!

Let's do unto them as we would do for others and ourselves!

Digging Deeper

How can we better use the "Golden Rule" within our family?

_____
_____
_____
_____
_____
_____
_____
_____
_____
_____
_____
_____
_____

Thoughts and prayers:

_____
_____
_____
_____
_____
_____
_____
_____
_____
_____
_____
_____
_____

"Here is a simple, rule-of-thumb guide for behavior: Ask yourself what you want people to do for you, then grab the initiative and do it for them."
Matthew 7:12 (MSG)

Day Twenty-Eight
Anxiety

Teen Jake

I feel most anxious before taking Chemistry tests!!! What makes you anxious??

Even though the Bible tells us to "Be anxious for nothing," the reality is feelings/anxiety will come! Whether it's when you are taking a test, like me, or when you walk into a room of people you do not know. Maybe for you it's stepping up to bat or walking out on the stage. It could be that anxiety comes from home and whatever issues may be stirring around.

No matter when those feelings come, it's a matter of how we respond to them that is most important and can bring peace the fastest.

The thing that brings peace the fastest for me is to stop and **realize** that anxiety is not from God. It can be real, but is really not meant to rule us. 2 Timothy 1:7 says, *"For God has not given us a spirit of fear, but of power and of love and of a sound mind."* If you struggle with anxiety, maybe you can write this scripture down and post it around, on your bathroom mirror, in your locker or in your car.

The second step for me is to **PRAY**. When I sit down to take that test and feel myself getting anxious, I simply say, "Holy Spirit come help me and guide me, bring to my memory what is needed for this test."

Finally, *I thank God* that He hears me, that He is with me and that through Him I can do all things! It's amazing how fast anxiety will leave and peace will come when I just ask for His help!

Mom Moment

Anxiety!!! That big A in the room, that sometimes lingers like a nine-hundred-pound gorilla!

What's a girl, what's a Mom to do with things such as social anxieties, fears, and challenges of all kinds in this life? You may have everything going peachy right now, or you may be a single mom struggling to pay the bills. You may be a mom sitting in St. Jude Children's Hospital fighting for your child's life or you may be a grandmother raising your grandchildren.

Anxiety is rooted in fear! It's fear of failure, fear of rejection, fear of the unknown… Fear in general is a paralyzing factor that can put anyone over the edge into anxiety.

Here is a little acronym that you may have heard for fear:

False
Evidence
Appearing
Real

Fear, for the most part, is false evidence appearing real. Did you know that ninety-nine percent of the stuff we worry about never comes to pass?

My husband, Alan, who is also Faith's dad, has his Masters in Marriage and Family counseling. Oftentimes, he counsels utilizing "Cognitive Behavior Therapy", its goal is to change patterns of thinking or behavior that are behind people's difficulties, which will change the way they feel. Does that sound a little like "renewing your mind?" (Romans 12:2) The Bible is so cool that it contains every answer we need!!!

As moms, leading our children, one of the greatest things we can do to help our children overcome anxiety is to introduce them to the solutions found in scripture! Whether it's the one Faith shared on fear or finding the very one that is the redemptive promise to the issue they are facing! Then lead them in a life of prayer and application. Then we can truly stand and say we are "anxious for nothing!"

Digging Deeper

During this prayer and thought time, allow yourself to be open and honest with God about the things that bring on anxiety in your relationship together and in other areas of life.

Seek God and His word, pray and feel His peace flood your life!

_____
_____
_____
_____
_____
_____
_____
_____
_____
_____
_____
_____
_____
_____
_____
_____
_____
_____
_____
_____
_____
_____
_____
_____
_____
_____
_____

Be anxious for nothing. But in everything by prayer and supplication, with thanksgiving, let your requests be made known to God; and the peace of God, which surpasses all understanding, will guard your hearts and minds through Christ Jesus.
Philippians 4:6-72

Day Twenty-Nine
God's Got It

Teen Take

In this chapter of Corinthians, Paul is talking about "the thorn in his flesh." He talks about how he begged God, more than once to take it away, but each time God said that His grace and power were sufficient. Through this trial, he learned to boast in his weakness so that Christ's power would be exalted.

Sometimes God allows us to go through trying times so that we can learn as Paul did. We cannot do this life by ourselves, and we weren't made to.

God's grace and power are always there, even when we are too blind or prideful to see it.

We can rest in the assurance that even though there may be a "thorn in our flesh," such as:

- An annoying sibling.
- A difficult subject at school.
- That bully.
- Drama with a group of friends.
- A chronic illness.
- Or a family matter.

Whatever that "thing" is, God can get us through it no matter what. Just ask Him for help! Remember when we are weak; He is strong in and through us!

Mom Moment

"Weakness" is not a word that our world looks at very keenly. From athletics to academics, from physical stature to intellect, the "world's" view is "only the strong survive." However, "weakness" from God's perspective is a completely different view!

Weakness from heaven's perspective is simply an opportunity for God to show Himself strong in and through us!

As a teenager or a parent or grandparent, in any season of life, we have God's promise of help. Whether our weakness is a physical issue, a runaway mouth (gossip), or a drug addiction, the completed work of our JESUS provides the help we need in the reality of our weaknesses.

We find an assurance of this in Hebrews 4:14-16 (NKJV)

*"Seeing then that we have a great High Priest who has passed through the heavens, Jesus the Son of God, let us hold fast our confession. For we do not have a High Priest who cannot sympathize with our weaknesses, but was in all points tempted as we are, yet without sin. Let us therefore **come boldly** to the throne of grace that we may **obtain mercy and find grace to help in time of need**."*

"Knowing" that when we are weak, He is strong and "knowing" He is there to help is one thing, but putting feet and action to that when we are in the midst of those times is another thing.

Based on these key scriptures here is God's action plan for our success amidst weaknesses ...

- Accept that there is no shame in weakness! We are not Jesus (perfect)!
- Accept His Grace (unmerited, undeserved favor).
- Go boldly (not begging) to God and ask for the help needed (you are His child and wouldn't you give your child the help needed?).
- Accept the help (God may give you instruction or He may literally send someone to help - accept it! Don't let pride keep you from His best).
- Remember - HE is strong when we are weak - GOD'S GOT IT!

Digging Deeper

Are there areas of your life that you feel "less than" (weakness)?

_____
_____
_____
_____
_____
_____
_____
_____

Have you let pride keep you from accepting help in this area or simply admitting you can't do it alone?

_____
_____
_____
_____
_____
_____
_____
_____

Go boldly to our God and ask for the help needed! You don't have to be superwoman all the time!! Gods got it!

_____
_____
_____
_____
_____
_____
_____

Each time He said, "My grace is all you need. My power works best in weakness." So now I am glad to boast about my weaknesses, so that the power of Christ can work through me. That's why I take pleasure in my weakness, and in the insults, hardships, persecutions, and troubles that I suffer for Christ. For when I am weak, then I am strong.
2 Corinthians 12:9-10 (NLT)

Day Thirty
All In

Teen Jake

Day 30!!! You made it!!!!!

I hope that over the past thirty days, this devotional has truly helped you grow closer to God and to your mom! So now, the next step is to continue to do this very thing. Spend time reading the Bible, praying, and talking to your mom! Maybe the two of you can establish a morning or night routine where y'all can hang out and share what the Lord is doing in your life and whatever else is happening in your life.

Remember, God is crazy about you and He and your mom want your very best! So don't be afraid to be real with both of them, in doing so your relationships will THRIVE!

Trust the Lord with all of your heart, with all of your successes and all of your failures. The things that can trip us up are not as big as our God is!! Keep Him center of it all and your mom will also be there to help you through it all!! Remember to thank her!

> *"The greatest legacy one can pass on to one's children and grandchildren is not money or other material things accumulated in one's life, but rather a legacy of character and faith."* - Billy Graham

Mom Moment

To be all in, we must trust God!!!! As women, trust can be a huge issue for us. Especially if you have been lied to, cheated on, or maybe didn't have a great relationship with your earthly Father. BUT GOD IS FAITHFUL!!

We have spent thirty days, each of which I pray, has helped you grow in your walk and in relationship with your daughter. It's okay even at this point to say you have some uncertainties or areas needing help, we all do! Just because we are "the moms" doesn't mean we have it all together. In fact, we never really will until we stand before Jesus face to face!

But what we CAN have is a life that is sold out for Jesus, a life that is rooted and planted in His truths and a life that produces fruit, our children, who will grow to be healthy people in their own right.

Here is God's promise of how we can THRIVE throughout all of life!

> Blessed is the one
> who does not walk in step with the wicked
> or stand in the way that sinners take
> or sit in the company of mockers,
> but whose delight is in the law of the Lord,
> and who meditates on his law day and night.
> That person is like a tree planted by streams of water,
> which yields its fruit in season
> and whose leaf does not wither—
> whatever they do prospers.
>
> Psalm 1:1-3 (NIV)

Digging Deeper

Thoughts and prayers:
___
___
___
___
___
___
___
___

Can you commit to staying on your journey, growing in the Lord and in your relationship together?
___
___
___
___
___
___
___
___

If so, what is your plan?
___
___
___
___
___
___
___
___

Trust in the Lord with all your heart; do not depend on your own understanding. Seek His will in ALL you do, and he will show you which path to take. Don't be impressed with your own wisdom. Instead, fear the Lord and turn away from evil. Then you will have healing for your body and strength for your bones.
Proverbs 3:5-8 (NLT)

Continuing to Thrive

Thank you so much for going on this 30 day journey with us!

We wanted to take a moment and share with you what God did in our lives through the writing of this book.

As we began the experience of co-authoring a book together, it held its share of challenges! Although we knew that the Lord had called us to share with other moms and daughters, we in no way felt we actually have it together enough on every subject to "be an expert."

As I would pen words about setting an example, as we'd drive down the road I would find myself with some slight road rage the next day! Isn't that just life! The enemy attempted on several occasions to whisper in my ear that I was not qualified in several areas.

I have been walking with the Lord enough to know and recognize His voice vs. the voice of the enemy. So we would take many breaks, allow for times of prayer and have many others praying for us, we'd have candid discussion, worship and we would then take another leap of faith into His Amazing Grace! The reality is, we are simply another mother and daughter duo seeking to walk in His perfect ways in our own imperfection.

The purpose of this devotional is to inspire you to grow closer to God and to one another. With great gratitude, I can say that is exactly what the process of writing this did for us personally, as well! Isn't God just so good? Our hearts' desire was fulfilled in our desire to provide this for you, our sisters in Christ!

In Faith's words:

"We grew closer to each other because we had to spend time together to agree on the topics and scriptures. In doing so we would spend time in worship and prayer, and we searched out scriptures together. When we would spend time writing and then reading what each other had to say, it helped us better understand what we each felt about the topic."

Putting those thoughts and feelings on paper first also gave us the opportunity to talk about things we previously had not. Our communication with each other has grown through our sitting down together and purposefully writing each one of the thirty day entries.

As for growing closer to God, when I would actually have to write down my thoughts or experiences, it helped me to see areas I need to continue to work on in my own relationship with Jesus. This challenged me to reflect and make sure that I am 'walking the walk' and not just 'talking the talk.'"

We encourage you to continue to make time for this very important part of your relationship. Spend time in worship and prayer together, read and study His Word and have conversation with one another. Be that safe place for each other to share, without fear of judgment or repercussions.

Look around to see if there may be another mother/daughter duo that this journey would also be a blessing to.

Also, we would love to stay connected with you! This Book is just the beginning! We are planning online and in person events to help you to continue to grow and keep our own relationship flourishing!

So please subscribe at **www.tinatatum.com**, find us on Facebook at Tina Tatum Ministries and on Instagram **@thrivetheministry**.

When you're talking on social media about how great you are doing as a result of this book bringing you closer in relationship with one another and with the Lord, please use our hashtag **#30days2thrive**.

Many blessings to you as you continue to Thrive!

Tina and Faith

About the Authors

Faith Tatum is a creative girl who enjoys painting, drawing, writing or just about any art you can imagine. But most of all she loves to hang out with God. Faith believes not only in strengthening her relationships with friends and family, but more importantly to set a godly example in those relationships. Faith has two amazing parents, one brother and 3 dogs, Skamp, Sadie and Lt Dan that bring her much joy.

Tina Tatum believes that we are called to live by design and not default! With a goal to inspire, encourage and equip women to be all that they are created to be! She is a minister of The Gospel and an Advocate for Freedom and Justice. She is founder of Tina Tatum Ministries, RefresHER and Thrive. She and her husband, Alan, are co-founders of R3 The Movement called to reach, rescue and redeem. Tina is the mother of the afore mentioned Faith Marie, and bonus son Kyle LaRue.

www.ingramcontent.com/pod-product-compliance
Lightning Source LLC
LaVergne TN
LVHW051556070426
835507LV00021B/2607